D1711957

WITHDRAWN
BY
WILLIAMSBURG REGIONAL LIBRARY

The Moon

by Heather Miller

KIDHAVEN PRESS

An imprint of Thomson Gale, a part of The Thomson Corporation

THOMSON

™

GALE

JUL - 2008

Detroit • New York • San Francisco • New Haven, Conn. • Waterville, Maine • London

WILLIAMSBURG REGIONAL LIBRARY
7770 CROAKER ROAD
WILLIAMSBURG, VIRGINIA 23188

© 2008 Thomson Gale, a part of The Thomson Corporation.

Thomson and Star Logo are trademarks and Gale and KidHaven Press are registered trademarks used herein under license.

For more information, contact
KidHaven Press
27500 Drake Rd.
Farmington Hills, MI 48331-3535
Or you can visit our Internet site at http://www.gale.com

ALL RIGHTS RESERVED.
No part of this work covered by the copyright hereon may be reproduced or used in any form or by any means—graphic, electronic, or mechanical, including photocopying, recording, taping, Web distribution or information storage retrieval systems—without the written permission of the publisher.

Every effort has been made to trace the owners of copyrighted material.

LIBRARY OF CONGRESS CATALOGING-IN-PUBLICATION DATA

Miller, Heather.
  The moon / Heather L. Miller.
    p. cm. — (Kidhaven science library)
  Includes bibliographical references and index.
  ISBN 978-0-7377-3777-6 (hardcover)
  1. Moon—Juvenile literature. I. Title.
  QB582.M55 2008
  523.3—dc22
 	
                                                                  2007022033

ISBN-10: 0-7377-3777-8

Printed in the United States of America

Contents

Chapter 1

Meet the Moon

The Moon is the second largest and brightest object in the daytime sky. Only the Sun is bigger and bolder. At night, the Moon is by far the most magnificent heavenly body that can be seen from Earth. Sometimes the Moon appears full and brilliant white. Other times, especially when its glow is softened by clouds, the Moon can look spooky and mysterious. From Earth, the Moon can appear very large at some times and very small at others. The Moon can glow yellow, orange, or even red. Sometimes the Moon brings only a tiny sparkle to the sky as it takes on the shape of a thin sliver. There are also nights when the Moon cannot be seen at all.

Seen or unseen, however, the Moon is always there. And although it may sometimes appear small, the Moon is enormous. It has a diameter of 2,160 miles (3,476km). That is about one-fourth the Earth's diameter and just less than the distance from Los Angeles, California, to Chicago, Illinois.

For centuries, observers on Earth have watched the giant rock known as the Moon. Some early people thought the Moon was a god sent to watch over Earth. Others assumed the spots of dark color seen on the Moon were oceans. Some stories even told that the Moon was made of cheese! Modern scientists and astronauts have learned a great deal about the Moon through exploration and study. Today, the mysteries of the Moon have started to unravel as scientists continue to learn more. Even so, there are still many unanswered questions to ponder and many mysteries to solve.

The Moon appears to change color from silver to red during a lunar eclipse.

Where Did the Moon Come From?

One of the biggest questions scientists wonder about is how the Moon was created. Scientists have proposed four main theories. The fission, sister planet, capture, and impact theories all explain the Moon's origin in very different ways.

Fission Theory

The fission theory states that the Moon was created from a piece of liquefied rock that split away from the Earth. Scientists who support this theory believe that early Earth was made up of rock so hot

Scientists theorize that at one time Earth rotated so fast on its axis that it assumed an elongated, oval shape.

it remained in a constant liquid state. Some believe at that time the Earth rotated on its axis at a speed much faster than today. These scientists claim the Earth rotated so fast that its days were just over two hours long! The strong forces created by this amazing speed caused the liquid Earth to change its shape from a ball to a more elongated, or oval, shape, similar to a bowling pin. Over time, the elongated end was thrown off into space. The released material eventually hardened into solid rock and became the Moon.

While this theory is interesting, most scientists do not agree with it. They argue that the extreme conditions necessary to cause such a dramatic event are nearly impossible. These same scientists also claim that if this theory were true, the soil and rocks found on the Moon would be more like the soil and rock found on the Earth. In fact, the Moon is made up of materials that are similar to, yet different from, those found on Earth.

Sister Planet Theory

A second theory suggests that the Earth and the Moon formed at the same time from the same collection of space material. The sister planet theory suggests that a cloud of dust, gases, and rock drifted into the **orbit** of the Sun. These materials began to clump together and over time formed two new objects: the Earth and the Moon.

Just as with the fission theory, scientists point out that if the sister planet theory were true, the composition of the soil and rocks on the Earth would be very similar to those on the Moon. Most scientists do not agree with the sister planet theory and have continued their search for a more reasonable explanation.

Capture Theory

A third explanation of the Moon's origin is described by the capture theory. Scientists who support the capture theory claim that the Moon was once a planet lost in space. This drifting planet happened to wander so close to the Earth's gravitational pull that it was captured and sent into orbit around the Earth.

While the fission theory and sister planet theory do not explain why the composition of the Moon and the Earth are so different, the capture theory does. If the Moon were once a planet from another part of the universe, it would most likely be composed of rocks and soil very different from the Earth's. But scientists still question the capture theory. They point out that the drifting planet would have been moving at a high rate of speed and would have most likely crashed into the Earth. Scientists have a difficult time explaining how the Moon could have slowed down just enough to slip into the Earth's orbit.

Debris trapped in the Sun's orbit might have formed the Earth and the Moon.

Impact Theory

The impact theory may provide the answer. Rather than describing a drifting planet that was captured by Earth's gravity, the impact theory suggests that a lost planet crashed into Earth at a very high rate of speed. When this planet hit Earth, the force of the crash was so great that the wandering planet melted and broke into pieces. Because early Earth

The Moon might once have been a drifting planet that was sucked into Earth's orbit by gravity.

The Moon

was made of liquid rock, the impact sent a huge splash of molten material from both planets shooting into space. Slowly, the orbiting ring of melted rock gathered into a ball shape. As it cooled, it became the Moon.

The impact theory is the one accepted by most scientists. Because the theory states that the Moon was created from parts of a foreign planet along with parts of Earth, it makes sense that the Moon's

Like the erupting Mount Etna (pictured), a planetary crash might have sent molten rock into space to form the Moon.

soil and rocks would be both different from and similar to Earth's. The theory also seems most likely to be true simply because it is not unusual for two space objects to crash into one another. But like all theories, the impact theory will have to be studied and tested for many years before it can be considered a fact. New tests and studies may reveal information to suggest an entirely new theory to describe how the Moon was formed. The mystery of the Moon's origin may never be completely solved.

Chapter 2

Geological Wonder

While the Moon is believed to be over 4.6 billion years old, modern science has just begun to uncover its secrets. The Moon is a mysterious place. It is completely dry, yet it has no air. The Moon has no wind, yet at night it is colder than anyplace on Earth. On the Moon the sky is always dark, yet from Earth the Moon appears to glow in the night sky. The Moon travels around the Earth, yet we see only one side of the Moon.

The Moon's surface provides scientists with a detailed illustration of billions of years of geological history. Scientists study the Moon's surface to discover evidence of ancient meteor impacts and volcanic eruptions. Scientists also study the Moon to help explain Earth's own history. While the Moon presents many mysteries, it is also a valuable source of scientific information.

Just as animal fossils help scientists learn about ancient life forms, the surface of the Moon is a collection of landforms that can reveal information about the history of the universe. Landforms such as **craters**, **basins**, mountains, and **rilles** cover the surface of the Moon. Each one of these landforms was created in a different way, and each explains a different piece of geological history.

Craters

From Earth, the Moon appears to be covered by great spans of light and dark areas. The early scientist Galileo suggested that the dark patches on

Mountain ranges and low spots covered by rocky soil create light and dark areas on the Moon's surface.

the Moon were vast seas of water. Today scientists know that most of the dark patches on the Moon are nothing more than low spots covered with rocky soil. Most of the areas of the Moon that appear light are covered by rugged mountains.

The most numerous geological features covering the Moon are craters. Craters appear as circular dents or impressions in the Moon's surface. Craters can be very large or very, very small. The Moon's surface has an estimated 3 trillion craters with diameters greater than 3 feet (1m). While 3 trillion is a huge number, it is dwarfed by the endless number of small craters that speckle the Moon's surface. Some Moon craters are as small as 1/25,000 inch (1/1000mm) across. That is about the size of a speck of dust.

These tiny craters were actually created by specks of cosmic dust. As tiny cosmic particles collided with the Moon, small indentations, or craters, were left behind in the Moon's fine, powdery soil. Large craters were created in a similar way. Meteorites, or large rocks flying through space, slammed against the Moon's surface. Because meteorites travel at such a high rate of speed, when they hit the Moon, the Moon's surface was pressed down and sideways. This powerful impact sent shock waves through both the meteorite and the Moon. The shock waves created an intense heat that vaporized parts of both objects. Lunar soil and parts of the meteorite were scattered out from the impact site in a shower of crumbled rock. The great force also caused a wave of rock to splash up from the impact site, creating a rim of rock and soil around the impact cavity. During this stage of creation, the impact cavity was tens of times larger than the meteorite that hit the Moon in the first place. As the energy calmed, the newly formed crater settled into a wider, shallower depression. As time passed, parts of the crater walls crumbled down and settled on the crater's floor.

Scientists who study craters have found bits of glass in samples taken from the bottoms of average-sized craters. This glass was formed as rock melted from the intense heat created by the impact of the meteorite. Larger craters, ranging from 9 to 31 miles (15–50km) across, were affected by even higher extreme temperatures. The surfaces of craters this size are often layered with a coating of melted meteorite material that has hardened over time.

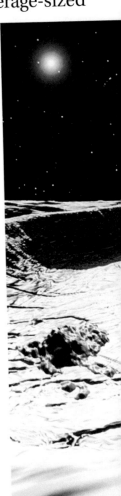

Basins

Moon craters can be extremely large, but basins are even larger. Basins are considered the largest class of impact craters. With diameters that range from 186 to 1,553 miles (300–2,500km) across, basins can make even the largest impact craters seem small.

Theories suggest that basins were formed in much the same way as impact craters. Scientists are limited in their study of lunar basins. All but a few lunar basins were filled by lava flows that seeped up through the Moon's crust, sealing valuable information away under layers of hardened rock. Scientists do know that the impact needed to

The surface of the Moon is covered with many lunar basins, the largest class of impact craters.

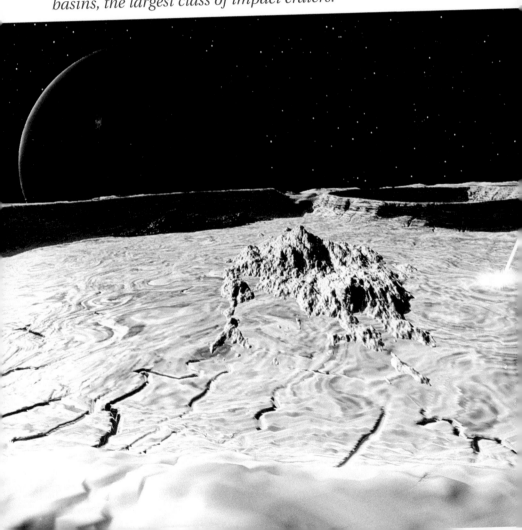

create lunar basins is great. In fact, the material ejected from the impact that created the Orientale Basin, one of the large basins on the Moon, was scattered over half the Moon's surface.

Mountains

Jagged peaks and mountain ranges are also features on the Moon's surface. Lunar mountain ranges are closely related to craters and basins. Most scientists agree that lunar mountain ranges are actually

Earth's tallest mountain, Mount Everest, is just slightly taller than the peaks of the Leibnitz Mountain range on the Moon.

the remaining ridges of craters that were filled entirely by lava flows. Near the Moon's South Pole, the Leibnitz mountain range rises 26,000 feet (7,920m) high. The tallest mountain on Earth, Mount Everest, stands 29,035 feet (8,850m) high, just 3,000 feet (930m) taller than the Leibnitz range.

Rilles

While lunar mountain ranges rise high above the Moon's surface, lunar formations called rilles, or valleys, dig down into the Moon's crust. The Ariadaeus Rille is a typical one, made up of a flat floor and sheer, straight walls. At about 3 miles (5km) wide, the Ariadaeus Rille is of average width. It is about 0.5 miles (0.8km) deep and stretches over 137 miles (220km). Scientists believe that the Ariadaeus Rille formed when the surface tension of the Moon reached a point where two parallel **faults**, or cracks, began to form. These two faults pulled apart until the rock and soil between them fell below the Moon's surface. There are rilles that cut through craters, mountain valleys, and even mountain ranges. They are yet another example of the fascinating geological formations that make up the Moon.

Moon Soil

Besides craters, basins and mountain ranges, and rilles, scientists also study the Moon's soil and rocks.

Most Moon rocks are made up of minerals that are found on Earth as well, including aluminum, calcium, iron, and magnesium.

Moon rocks can be divided into two categories, **basalt** and **breccia**. Basalt rocks are made from lava that was once hot and fluid but has since cooled. Because so many basalt rocks have been found on the Moon, scientists know that at one time the Moon was extremely hot and went through periods with high volcanic activity. Breccia rocks are made up of soil and smaller rocks. Scientists say breccia rocks were formed when meteorites bom-

This table shows the composition of lunar meteorites, products of the Moon's soil and other substances.

Lunar Meteorites		
Name	**Rock Type**	**Where Found**
ALHA81005	Highlands breccia	Antarctica, Transantarctic Mountains
Y-791197	Highlands breccia	Antarctica, Yamato Mountains
Y-793169	Basalt	Antarctica, Yamato Mountains
Y-793274	Basalt breccia	Antarctica, Yamato Mountains
Y-82192, Y-82193, Y-86032	Highlands breccia	Antarctica, Yamato Mountains
EET87521	Basalt breccia	Antarctica, Transantarctic Mountains
MAC88104, MAC88105	Highlands breccia	Antarctica, Transantarctic Mountains
Asuka-881757	Basalt	Antarctica, Yamato Mountains Area
Calcalong Creek	Highlands breccia	Nullarbor Plain, South Australia
QUE93069, QUE94269	Highlands breccia	Antarctica, Transantarctic Mountains
QUE94281	Basalt breccia	Antarctica, Transantarctic Mountains

Billions of years ago, volcanic activity on the Moon helped shape the surface of the Moon as it exists today.

barded the Moon. These objects squeezed soil and rock together with such force that the process created new breccia rocks.

Regolith, or lunar soil, is another product that resulted from the continuous impact of meteorites. With each impact, lunar rocks were broken down into smaller and smaller particles until finally, dusty particles of regolith covered the Moon. A layer of regolith approximately 60 feet (20m) deep covers the surface of the Moon.

Unlike the soil on Earth, lunar soil does not contain organic material, oxygen, or water. Because of the lack of these building blocks of life, it is impossible to grow plants in lunar soil or support life on the Moon.

The Moon may be a quiet, desolate place today, but billions of years ago it was affected by dramatic geological activity. Meteorites and volcanic activity produced craters, basins, mountain ranges, and rilles, as well as lunar rocks and soil. The Moon's history is filled with stories of explosions and crashes, all waiting to be discovered by the scientists who study its surface.

Chapter 3

The Moon and Earth

While there may not be life on the Moon, the Moon affects billions of lives each day. Throughout history, the Moon has influenced humans in many ways. Along with casting a glowing light that helps humans see in the dark, the Moon has influenced how people keep track of time and also affects the level of the Earth's oceans.

As the Earth's closest celestial neighbor, the Moon has an important relationship with the planet. The Moon travels around Earth in an oval-shaped path called an orbit. The Moon orbits Earth about 238,857 miles (384,403km) above the planet, and travels about 2,300 miles (3,700km) per hour.

Although the Moon appears to glow, it does not produce its own light. The light that seems to come from the Moon is actually sunlight reflected off the Moon's surface. At any given time, one-half of the Moon's surface is illuminated by the Sun. But because the Moon orbits the Earth, there are times when the planet's shadow hides part of the Moon, and humans cannot see its entire illuminated surface. Depending

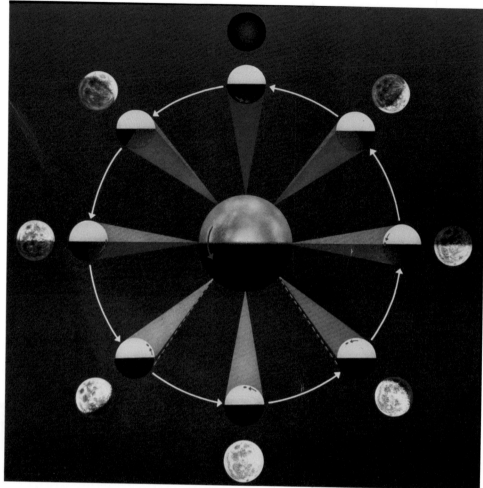

The Moon's orbital path determines the shape of the Moon that is seen from Earth.

on where the Moon is in its orbital path, it can appear as a half-circle, a crescent, or a thin sliver. These different Moon shapes are called **phases**.

During the Moon's first phase, or New Moon, it cannot be seen at all. After the New Moon phase, the Moon begins to appear as a small illuminated crescent. This phase is called the Waxing Crescent.

Days later, the part of the Moon that can be seen increases to a half-circle shape. This phase is called the First Quarter. As days pass, more and more of the Moon becomes visible until it finally glows in the sky as a full circle. This phase is called a Full Moon. After the Full Moon phase, the amount of Moon seen from Earth begins to decrease. During the Last Quarter phase, the Moon once again appears as a half circle. In a few days the Moon again looks crescent shaped as it enters the Waning Crescent phase. The crescent of glowing light decreases to a smaller and smaller sliver until finally the Moon is invisible, and another New Moon phase begins.

The Moon looks crescent-shaped at the beginning of its orbital path, known as the Waxing Crescent, and again toward the end of its orbital path, known as the Waning Crescent.

It takes about 29.5 days for the Moon to make one full **revolution**, or complete trip around the Earth. It is on the revolution of the Moon that humans have based the twelve-month calendar. But because one Moon revolution takes just less than thirty days, the Moon phase at the beginning of the month usually repeats itself again at the very end of the month. Sometimes, two Full Moons occur in a single month. When this occurs, approximately every three years, the second Full Moon is called a **Blue Moon**.

Ocean Tides

The Moon affects more than just the way people keep track of the months. It also has a great effect on the Earth's surfaces. The gravitational attraction caused by the Moon as the Earth rotates is so strong that it actually moves the Earth's water. The Moon's gravitational forces, along with the centrifugal forces created by the spinning Earth, cause the Earth's water to move as one large mass of liquid. On the side of the Earth closest to the Moon, the water is pulled up into a hump, or bulge, by the Moon's gravity. At the same time, the opposite side of the Earth also experiences a bulge of water. Because the Moon is far away from the opposite side, the Moon's pull on that side is weak, allowing the Earth's centrifugal force to spin the water up into another bulge.

At locations on Earth where the ocean bulges, a **high tide** occurs. As the tide moves in, the ocean level rises and the water slowly moves up the shore. What was a sandy beach is slowly covered with water. At the peak of high tide, the shoreline of some coastal areas can be pushed back nearly a mile.

While most coastal areas experience slow tidal transitions, a few places on Earth experience sudden changes. Some bays, such as the Bay of Fundy, located between New Brunswick and Nova Scotia, experience a powerful and forceful arrival of high tide called a **tidal bore**. At the Bay of Fundy, tidal bores arrive as fast-moving walls of water. Tidal bores can move at a rate of 22 miles (35km) per

The Bay of Fundy experiences low tides, pictured, and powerful high tides.

hour and can bring in a wall of water more than 10 feet (3.04m) tall.

While high tide is happening in some coastal areas, other locations experience **low tide**. Low tide happens in areas where the water is being pulled away from the shore. During low tide, the ocean level seems to decrease. At the shoreline the ocean's water level gets shallower, and beach visitors may venture out to discover tidal pools, shells, and creatures that are normally covered by water.

The Earth experiences two tidal cycles each day. Each tidal cycle occurs approximately twelve and one-half hours from the last. Because the positions of the Moon and the Earth change each day, so do the tides. There are times during the year when the tides are higher than others. When the Moon and Sun are on the same side of the Earth at the same time, their gravitational forces are combined. As a result, the tides are much higher. This type of extreme high tide is called a spring tide. Whether the Moon is full or new or the tide is high or low, day and night, the Earth is constantly affected by the Moon.

Eclipses

There are also certain times when the Earth has an unusual effect on the Moon—the Moon is completely shaded by the dark shadow of the Earth. This phenomenon is called a lunar eclipse. During a lunar eclipse the Earth passes between the Sun and the Moon, blocking the Sun's light and casting a shadow over the Moon. This is much like a shadow being cast from a child walking on a sidewalk. When the child stands between the Sun and a butterfly resting on the sidewalk, the child's body blocks the Sun's light and casts a shadow on the butterfly. The butterfly is still visible, but it is darkened by the shadow of the child. If the child were

During a lunar eclipse the Earth passes between the Sun and the Moon, which leaves the Moon in a shadow.

During a solar eclipse the Moon comes between the Sun and the Earth.

to stand still, the angle of the Sun would soon shift as the Earth turns, and the butterfly would again be fully in the Sun's light.

During a lunar eclipse the full, brightly glowing Moon is slowly covered by the Earth's shadow. At the peak of a lunar eclipse, the Moon appears to be shaded and most often looks dim and gray. But soon, as the Earth rotates, the Sun's light is once again reflected off of the Moon's surface, and the Moon again appears to glow brightly.

Just as during a lunar eclipse the Earth blocks the Sun's light from reaching the Moon, there are also times when the Moon blocks the Sun's rays from reaching the Earth. This type of eclipse is called a solar eclipse. During a solar eclipse, the Moon passes directly between the Sun and the Earth and most of the Sun's rays are blocked from reaching Earth. At its most striking moment, when the Moon is perfectly centered between the Earth and Sun, a brilliant ring of light appears around the darkened Sun. This ring is actually the Sun's atmosphere, or **corona**.

During a solar eclipse the phenomenon can only be seen in certain parts of the world. Only those areas that lie in the direct path of the Moon's shadow will experience a solar eclipse. This path, also called the path of totality, is never more than 170 miles (274km) wide. On average, solar eclipses last for only about two and a half minutes. Even though the moment is short, it is an exciting and unusual event anticipated and enjoyed by many people.

While some people look forward to watching eclipses, many others are content simply to watch the Moon each night as it passes through its many phases. Wherever one travels on Earth, the night sky showcases a familiar friend—Earth's natural satellite, the Moon.

Chapter 4

Exploring the Moon

Long ago, humans could only wonder and dream as they stared up at the Moon. Stories of the Moon included descriptions of great oceans and aliens, of mystery and great power. Today, scientists have a much better idea of how the Moon was created and what it is made of. Scientists and special robots have traveled into space to collect samples and take photographs of the Moon. These exploration programs have helped scientists learn a great deal.

Many countries have sent rockets and satellites into space. The first countries to explore the Moon were the Soviet Union and the United States. Several attempts were made before a successful mission was accomplished. On August 17, 1958, the United States made its first attempt to send up a lunar probe, which was called the *Pioneer*. The *Pioneer* exploded before it could enter space. After two more failed attempts by the United States, the Soviet Union launched the *Luna 1* into space on January 2, 1959. The *Luna 1* managed to fly within 3,700

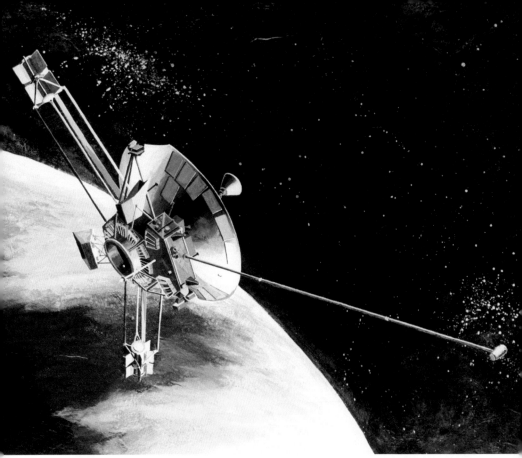

The first Pioneer *spacecraft failed to reach the Moon but later versions, such as* Pioneer 10 *(pictured), succeeded.*

miles (6,000km) of the Moon before being swept up by the solar wind. On March 3, 1959, the United States successfully sent its first lunar probe into space as the *Pioneer 4* moved even closer than *Luna 1* to the Moon before being sent into solar orbit.

The first spacecraft to arrive on the Moon was sent by the Soviet Union. On September 14, 1959, the *Luna 2* made the first hard, or crash, landing on the Moon. One month later, the Soviet Union sent the *Luna 3* to take the first pictures of the far side of the Moon. For the next several years both the United States and the Soviet Union made many more failed attempts to reach the Moon. Five years passed before another important event in Moon exploration. On July 31, 1964, the U.S. probe *Ranger 7* sent back the first close-range pictures of the Moon. The following year *Ranger 8*, equipped with six television cameras, sent back more than 7,000 crisp, clear photographs of the Moon.

Many different lunar modules have landed on the Moon since 1959.

Both the United States and the Soviet Union worked hard to develop a spacecraft that could land softly on the Moon. Landing softly would allow equipment to be sent to the Moon's surface without being destroyed. In January 1966 the Soviet craft *Luna 9* made the first successful soft landing on the Moon. The *Luna 9* returned the first photographs of the Moon taken from the Moon's surface.

Humans Walk on the Moon

Although making the first soft landing on the Moon was a huge step forward in the advancement of Moon exploration, the most extraordinary event by far was achieved by the United States and *Apollo 11*. On July 16, 1969, *Apollo 11* was launched from the Kennedy Space Center in Florida. The spacecraft carried three astronauts—Neil Armstrong, Edwin Aldrin, and Michael Collins. The astronauts flew toward the Moon for three days before they reached their targeted close-range orbit.

While orbiting the Moon at close range, Armstrong and Aldrin crawled into the lunar module, which would take them to the surface of the Moon. Collins stayed aboard *Apollo* to operate the control panel. The lunar module landed in a smooth, low area of the Moon called the Sea of Tranquility. On July 20, 1969, Armstrong became the first person to set foot on the Moon.

Less than six months later, a second successful mission sent two more astronauts to the Moon. In November 1969, Charles Conrad Jr. and Alan L. Bean brought 76 pounds (34.4kg) of samples of Moon material back to Earth for study. Between 1969 and 1972, the United States sent a total of six astronaut crews to the Moon's surface.

Apollo 11 astronaut Edwin "Buzz" Aldrin (pictured) was the second person to walk on the Moon.

Lunar roving vehicles allowed astronauts to travel farther on the Moon and gather more data for scientific experiments.

On all these missions, the astronauts gathered samples and conducted experiments. On one mission, astronauts planted a device to measure seismic activity, or movement of the Moon's crust. Later, other astronauts sent discarded space "junk" crashing into the Moon's surface to see how the

Moon's crust would react. Other missions involved drilling into the Moon's crust, gathering samples of soil and rock, and launching small satellites. There have been no astronaut landings on the Moon since the *Apollo 17* mission of December 1972. During this mission Eugene A. Cernan and Harrison H. Schmitt spent more than 75 hours traveling more than 18 miles (30km) over the Moon's surface in a robotic vehicle known as a lunar rover.

Future Missions

While it may seem that interest in Moon exploration has faded since the 1970s, new missions are scheduled for the future. Several countries, including China, Japan, and the United States, have plans to return to the Moon. China plans to launch the *Chang'e 1*, a lunar exploratory probe. The *Chang'e 1* is scheduled to orbit the Moon from about 125 miles (210km) from its surface. The probe's mission will be to create a detailed map of the Moon's crust.

Japan also plans to kick off its own investigation of the Moon by launching that country's first lunar orbiter. The SELENE is a three-ton (2.7 metric ton) satellite equipped with two small subsatellites designed to gather scientific data from the Moon. The SELENE is scheduled for a one-year mission to study the elements and minerals on the Moon as well as its gravitational field. Japan and China also have plans to send lunar rovers to the Moon.

The United States is also continuing its Moon exploration program. On September 19, 2005, the National Aeronautics and Space Administration (NASA) announced plans to send astronauts back to the Moon by the year 2018. A new and improved spacecraft will be used. It is called the Crew

Europe, Japan, and China all have launch vehicles intended for exploring the Moon.

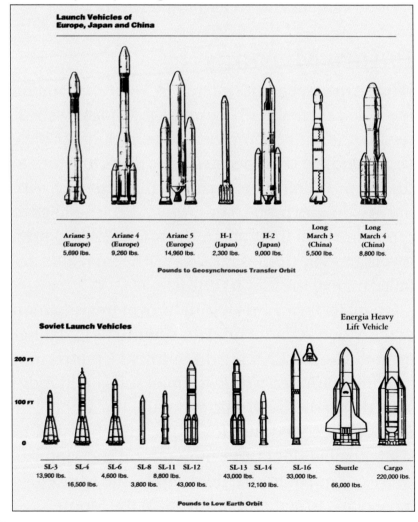

Launch Vehicles of
Europe, Japan and China

| Ariane 3 (Europe) 5,690 lbs. | Ariane 4 (Europe) 9,260 lbs. | Ariane 5 (Europe) 14,960 lbs. | H-1 (Japan) 2,300 lbs. | H-2 (Japan) 9,000 lbs. | Long March 3 (China) 5,500 lbs. | Long March 4 (China) 8,800 lbs. |

Pounds to Geosynchronous Transfer Orbit

Soviet Launch Vehicles

Energia Heavy Lift Vehicle

| SL-3 13,900 lbs. | SL-4 16,500 lbs. | SL-6 8,800 lbs. | SL-8 3,800 lbs. | SL-11 | SL-12 43,000 lbs. | SL-13 43,000 lbs. | SL-14 12,100 lbs. | SL-16 33,000 lbs. | Shuttle 66,000 lbs. | Cargo 220,000 lbs. |

Pounds to Low Earth Orbit

Exploration Vehicle, or CEV, and is designed to carry six astronauts. NASA hopes to launch the first CEV into space by 2012.

The CEV is much bigger than the lunar modules carried by the *Apollo* missions, and unlike the *Apollo* craft, it is designed to be reused. It will hook up in space with a new lunar lander spacecraft that will take four astronauts to the Moon's surface. The new lunar lander will support missions up to a week long. Upon completing their assigned tasks on the Moon, the astronauts will return to the CEV, which will take them back to Earth.

The program brings a brand-new vision to the U.S. space program and its ability to explore the Moon. Only the future will tell what advances and discoveries may result from this renewed interest in lunar exploration.

basalt: A rock formed from hardened lava from a volcano.

basins: Very large depressions in the Moon's surface thought to be caused by meteorite impacts. Similar to craters but much larger.

Blue Moon: The second Full Moon phase to occur within the same month.

breccia: A rock made up of smaller rocks squeezed together by extreme heat and pressure.

corona: The outer atmosphere of the Sun.

craters: Bowl-shaped depressions in the Moon's surface caused by meteorite impacts.

faults: Breaks or cracks in the Moon's crust.

high tide: The coastal rise in ocean level caused by the gravitational pull of the Moon.

low tide: A decrease in water level at a coastline that occurs when the Earth's ocean water on other parts of the Earth is pulled into high tide by the Moon's gravitational pull.

orbit: The area around the Sun or the Earth that influences other heavenly bodies; the process of revolving around something; the path the Moon travels when it moves around the Earth.

phases: Changes in the Moon's appearance as it orbits the Earth.

regolith: Powdery soil on the Moon formed from constant bombardment of the Moon's crust by meteorites.

revolution: The movement of the Moon around the Earth. It takes the Moon about one month to complete one full revolution around the Earth.

rilles: Steep-walled lunar valleys caused by a drop in the Moon's crust along two fault lines.

tidal bore: An advancing high tide that arrives as a fast-moving wall of water.

For Further Exploration

Books

Franklyn M. Branley, *The Moon Seems to Change*. New York: Crowell, 1987. Part of the Let's Read and Find Out Science 2 series, this book uses simple terms to explain the Moon's phases.

Gail Gibbons, *The Moon Book*. New York: Holiday House, 1997. Learn how to make a solar eclipse viewer with this book, which explains the origin of the Moon, the phases of the Moon, and how the Moon creates tides and solar eclipses.

Michael Light, *Full Moon*. New York: Knopf, 2002. Filled with amazing photos of the Moon taken by NASA's *Apollo* missions, this book provides an up-close view of the distant Moon.

Web Sites

National Air and Space Museum (www.nasm.si.edu). Search for "Discover the Moon" to reveal a wide variety of topics including Moon phases and eclipses, and read the calendar to find out when the next Blue Moon will occur.

The Nine Planets (www.nineplanets.org). Scroll down and click on "Moon" to find dozens of Moon facts, photos, and links to other informative Web Sites.

The Planetary Society (www.planetary.org/explore/kids/). Check out this site to find pictures of early lunar impactors, check the Lunar Eclipse Chart to find out when you can observe the next lunar eclipse, or calculate how much you would weigh if you visited the Moon.

To the Moon, Nova Online (www.pbs.org/wgbh/nova/tothemoon). On this site sponsored by PBS, you can hear NASA astronauts tell about their experiences as they traveled to the Moon, look at photos taken on the Moon, and test your knowledge as you try to solve lunar puzzles.

World Book @ NASA (www.nasa.gov/worldbook/moon_worldbook.html). This site includes links to interesting student information, including "Earth, Moon, Mars, Beyond" and "Kids 3-2-1 Blastoff."

Index

Picture Credits

Cover photo: photos.com
AP Images, 5, 11, 17, 35
© CORBIS, 21
© Paul A. Souders/CORBIS, 27
© Alison Wright/CORBIS, 18
Paul and Lindamarie Ambrose/Taxi/Getty Images, 25
George Diebold/Photographer's Choice/Getty Images, 6
Ray Massey/Stone/Getty Images, 30
World Perspectives/Stone/Getty Images, 38
Time & Life Pictures/Getty Images, 34, 37
JLM Visuals, 14
Macmillan Library Reference, 20
Great Images in NASA, 10
David A. Hardy/Photo Researcher's, Inc., 24
Jerry Lodriguss/Photo Researcher's, Inc., 29
Steve A. Munsinger/Photo Researcher's, Inc., 9
U.S. National Aeronautics and Space Administration, 40

About the Author

Heather Miller is the author of over 35 books for children. She lives in northeast Indiana, where she spends her time reading, writing, and teaching art to children. As a young girl, she spent many nights watching the Moon as it crept across the sky over her favorite lake in Minnesota. She remembers sitting for hours, waiting to see her first lunar eclipse.